— Animal Trackers —
TRACKING ANIMAL
MOVEMENT

Tom Jackson

raintree
a Capstone company — publishers for children

Raintree is an imprint of Capstone Global Library Limited, a company incorporated in
England and Wales having its registered office at 7 Pilgrim Street, London EC4V 6LB
Registered company number 6695582

www.raintree.co.uk
myorders@raintree.co.uk

ISBN: 978-1-4747-0232-4

For Brown Bear Books Ltd:
Text: Tom Jackson
Designer: Lynne Lennon
Design Manager: Keith Davis
Editorial Director: Lindsey Lowe
Children's Publisher: Anne O'Daly
Picture Manager: Sophie Mortimer
Production Director: Alastair Gourlay

British Library Cataloguing in Publication Data
A full catalogue record for this book is available from the British Library.

Acknowledgements
t=top, c=centre, b=bottom, l=left, r=right

Front Cover: Flip Nicklin/Minden Pictures/FLPA
1, ©Barrett Hedges/Alamy; 4, ©Shane Gross/Shutterstock; 5, ©NCG/Shutterstock; 6, ©Sam D Cruz /Shutterstock;
7tr, ©Rockwell Aerospace; 7br, ©National Park Service; 8, ©Michelle Lalancette /Shutterstock; 9, ©Barrett Hedges/Alamy;
10, ©Ian Wray/Alamy; 11bl, ©Hemera/Thinkstock; 12, ©Gerry Ellis/Getty Images; 13, ©WENN Ltd/Alamy;
14, ©Paul Nicklen/Getty Images; 16 ©Isabelle Kuehn/Shutterstock; 17cl, ©Flip Nicklin/Minden Pictures/Corbis;
17tc, ©Phil Reid/Shutterstock; 18, ©Stephan Savoia/Associated Press; 19t, ©Markuso/Shutterstock;
19b, ©Elizabeeth Hoffmann/Thinkstock; 20, ©Dan Costa/University of California, Santa Cruz;
21, ©Nancy Nehring/Thinkstock; 22, ©Luna Vandoorne/Shutterstock; 23, ©D J Mattaar/Shutterstock;
24, ©GTS Production/Shutterstock; 25bl, ©Moizhusein/Shutterstock; 25bc, ©Mogens Trolle/Shutterstock;
25br, ©Bryan Busovicki/Shutterstock; 26c, ©Blue Point Conservation Science; 26b, ©Epantha/Thinkstock;
27, ©Genevieve Vallee/Alamy; 28, ©Dr. Darren Irwin; 29, ©NEXRAD/NOAA.

All Artworks © Brown Bear Books Ltd
Brown Bear Books has made every attempt to contact the copyright holder.
If anyone has any information please contact licensing@brownbearbooks.co.uk.

Some words are shown in bold, **like this**. You can find out
what they mean by looking at the glossary.

Printed in China
19 18 17 16 15
10 9 8 7 6 5 4 3 2 1

CONTENTS

WHY WE TRACK ANIMAL MOVEMENT

Most animals move to look for food, to find a mate and to find places to have their babies. Some animals move just a short distance. Others travel for thousands of kilometres. Scientists use tracking devices to record where animals go.

Trackers have revealed the places where sperm whales gather to breed every year. The rest of the time the whales live alone and are rarely seen.

RARE ANIMALS

There are many reasons to track animal movements. Endangered animals, like tigers and rhinoceroses, are very rare and hard to find in the wild. Fitting a tracker allows **biologists** to know where endangered animals can be found. Scientists can then make sure the places the animals travel to are kept protected.

FACT: Arctic terns fly 71,000 kilometres (44,000 miles) every year – further than any other animal.

MIGRATIONS

Many animals, such as whales and birds, migrate. That means they travel to new areas as the seasons change. Tracking shows us that migrating animals follow the same route each year. Scientists work to protect the places along the migration route because the animals are not able to travel another way.

BEHAVIOUR

Finally trackers help us to discover many interesting things about how animals behave. They can show us where they go to find their food – and when – and how they protect themselves from attack.

Millions of monarch butterflies fly south from North America to Mexico in autumn. They all spend the winter in the same woodland.

5

GPS AND RADIO

Animal trackers make use of the same tracking technology used in mobile phones, walkie-talkies and in-car **satellite navigation** systems. That allows scientists to follow animals minute-by-minute as they travel huge distances.

KEEPING UP

Scientists can't track every animal's movements simply by following it. This might make an animal stop behaving in a natural way. And some animals are too fast for people to keep up with. Instead scientists use trackers that send out signals.

These African cheetahs have radio trackers fitted to collars. Wearing the tracker is not uncomfortable and does not affect the cats at all.

USING SATELLITES

Satellite trackers use GPS (Global Positioning System), which is the same thing used by navigation systems in cars. The tracker picks up signals from satellites in the sky. The satellites send out the signals at the same time. Each signal travels a different distance to the tracker and arrives at a slightly different time. The tracker uses these differences to work out where it is. It then sends the result to scientists. Some trackers just use the mobile phone network. Others transmit data to another satellite, which passes it on to researchers.

An ARGOS satellite orbits Earth every 100 minutes, collecting data from trackers.

RADIO SIGNAL

Simple trackers send out radio signals, which are picked up by a receiver held by the researcher. This kind of signal does not travel as far as the GPS system. It does not give an exact position, but shows how far away the animal is, and in which direction it is moving.

REINDEER TRACKS

The information from a satellite tracker is displayed on a map like this one showing the journeys of reindeer in Alaska. The tracker can also show how fast the deer move.

—— fast —— slow

TRACKING GREY WOLVES

A wolf is built to run. It can travel 48 kilometres (30 miles) in a single day as it looks for food. We know this because of radio trackers. Radio trackers help scientists discover more information about wolf behaviour.

Wolves live in packs of about ten. The pack hunts together to kill large animals like deer, but wolves also hunt alone.

FITTING THE TRACKER

To fit a tracker, scientists first have to trap the wolf. They use a foot-trap, which grabs the animal by one leg. This does not hurt the wolf. Next an expert **sharpshooter** shoots the wolf with a dart, which makes the animal fall asleep. The scientists then fit a tracker attached to a neck collar. When the wolf wakes up, it can run away to rejoin its pack.

FOLLOW THE PACK

Most of the world's wolves live in North America, Scandinavia and Russia where there are vast areas of cold forest and mountains. Wolves move so far and fast through these areas that scientists have to follow them in aircraft.

Whenever a wolf is picked up by the radio receiver on board the aircraft, its tracker sends back information about how far the wolf has run in the last day. The same wolf may be tracked for several years as it grows up. Its tracker must be replaced from time to time. To do that scientists activate a drugged dart in the collar, which puts the animal to sleep for a few hours.

A wolf is darted from a helicopter. The dart is fired from a rifle. It puts a drug into the wolf's blood, which will make it fall asleep.

FACT: A young wolf was once tracked running for 800 kilometres (500 miles) as it looked for a new pack.

MIGRATING OSPREYS

Ospreys are fish-eating **birds of prey** that live all over the world. North American ospreys fly to South America in winter. Satellite trackers are used to show their migration routes.

OSPREY COUNTRY

The world's largest **population** of ospreys lives in the Chesapeake Bay area on the East Coast of the United States. Like ospreys around the world, numbers of these birds fell very quickly during the 1960s and the 1970s.

This osprey has a GPS tracker fitted to its back. The tracker is very light so the bird can fly – and hunt – as normal.

This was because chemicals used by farmers damaged the birds' eggs so fewer chicks were able to hatch. Osprey numbers are rising again, and to make sure they keep rising biologists use trackers to study where the birds go each year.

GPS TRACKERS

Ospreys from Chesapeake Bay are fitted with trackers that use GPS. The bird's tracker sends out its location every hour as it flies from North America to its wintering grounds in South America. This shows researchers the migration route the bird is taking, including where it stops to rest and hunt. That helps identify places where birds might need protecting from human hunters who do not like the birds taking fish.

JOIN IN

Tracking ospreys

Find out more about the Chesapeake Bay project and others like it by looking for these organisations online:

Chesapeake Bay Foundation
Rutland Ospreys Project
Royal Society for the Protection of Birds (RSPB)

Information from GPS trackers shows the different migration routes used by ospreys migrating between North and South America.

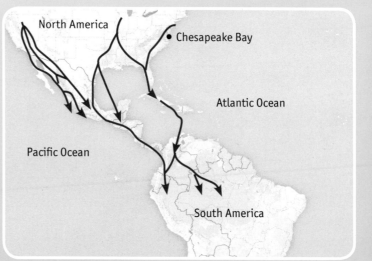

AMERICA: Osprey migration

North America

Chesapeake Bay

Atlantic Ocean

Pacific Ocean

South America

FOLLOWING
PANDAS

Giant pandas are one of the world's rarest animals. They live only in a few bamboo forests in southern China. Pandas need help breeding, and trackers are used to work out how they find mates.

BAMBOO BEAR

Scientists think there are just 1,000 panda bears left in the wild. The bears eat bamboo that grows in the mountains of China. Much of the bears' natural **habitat** has been cut down. Some bamboo forests are now protected, but the number of pandas is not going up. To find out why not, biologists use radio trackers to understand more about a panda's behaviour.

LIVING ALONE

Giant pandas are shy and live by themselves. They are easily scared by humans in the area.

This panda is marking a tree with its scent to communicate with other bears. A tracker around its neck helps researchers make a map of the bear's territory.

If two bears meet they will normally have a fight or just run away from each other. A female panda becomes ready to breed just once a year. She will only mate with a male if she does not feel scared. So researchers checking to see which pandas are breeding have to stay further away. Chinese scientists are using radio trackers to study the bears instead.

BREEDING WATCH

Radio trackers show that female pandas live in a **territory** of about 5 square kilometres (2 square miles). Males also have a territory of about the same size, but they regularly come into the areas of their female neighbours. The trackers show if a male and female are spending time together. That means they are mating, and researchers will look for a bear cub when the time is right.

Panda researchers regularly check the cubs for injuries and illness. They also take measurements of the pandas as they grow.

WOW!

To increase the panda population, scientists are raising pandas in zoos and releasing them into the wild. The researchers dress up in panda suits to stop the cubs from getting used to seeing humans. When the cubs are set free, they will be used to seeing pandas around and keep away from humans.

POLAR BEARS IN CANADA

The number of polar bears in the Arctic Ocean is falling. Scientists know that the bears have been affected by climate change and pollution. To understand the problem better, scientists need to know where the bears travel.

ARCTIC WANDERERS

Polar bears are not easy to track because they live in remote places. They walk for long distances over ice and can swim for hours in the cold water. Even if scientists could follow them in aircraft it would stop the bears from behaving naturally. GPS trackers are used to follow the bears **remotely**.

NECK COLLARS

Researchers fit collars with radio transmitters around the necks of bears. Signals from the collars are beamed to a satellite orbiting Earth.

A researcher fits a tracking collar to a polar bear in Canada. Bears are dangerous and researchers use a dart gun to make the bear fall asleep before going near.

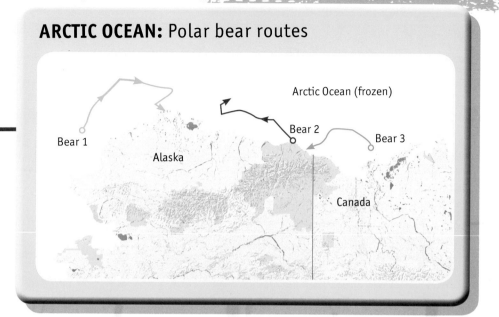

ARCTIC OCEAN: Polar bear routes

Arctic Ocean (frozen)

Bear 1

Bear 2

Bear 3

Alaska

Canada

The map shows the routes followed by polar bears north of Alaska in spring, when the ocean is completely frozen.

When a bear goes from one place to another, its movement is tracked by the satellite. The collar is fitted tightly because the bear will lose weight in winter and get a lot thinner – and it is important that the collar does not fall off.

CHANGING BEHAVIOURS

The Arctic is changing as the climate warms up. There is less ice covering the ocean, which is where the polar bears hunt. The trackers tell scientists how these changes affect the bears. They are interested to see where the bears go to hunt, if they come into towns to feed and when they stop to **hibernate** in snow dens. Over time this will show if the bears can adapt to the changes in the Arctic.

Follow polar bears

Researchers from Norway, Canada and the United States track the journeys made by polar bears across the frozen Arctic Ocean. Many of the results are shown on websites. Search for these organisations online to see the movements of polar bears tracked month by month:

Alaska Science Center, United States Geological Survey (USGS)

World Wide Fund for Nature (WWF), polar bear tracker

FACT: Trackers are only fitted to female bears. The males get so thin the collars drop off.

Protecting Sea Turtles

Loggerhead sea turtles are endangered. They face threats both at sea and while laying eggs on beaches. Trackers are being used to keep them safe.

While at sea, loggerhead turtles can be caught in fishing nets, hit by big ships or frightened away from feeding grounds by noisy tourists. The females visit beaches to lay their eggs – and are often too afraid to come on land.

Florida project

A tracker project on the east coast of Florida is trying to find the best way to protect the area's loggerheads. Researchers know that a female turtle will always come to the same beach to lay her eggs every two or three years. The scientists capture a female turtle after she lays eggs, and a tracker is fitted as quickly as possible so she can get back into the water the next day. There are currently 33 Florida loggerheads being tracked using GPS. When each one returns to its laying beach, the scientists will replace the tracker.

Loggerhead turtle

One of just seven species of sea turtle, loggerheads live in warm oceans all over the world. They eat shellfish and seaweed. The turtles are about 0.9 metre (3 feet) long and live for about 50 years.

On track

It is important to protect turtle beaches so that loggerheads can come back year after year to lay eggs. The tracker programme also shows the places out at sea where these rare turtles need protecting.

The tracker

A GPS tracker is carefully glued to the turtle's hard shell. Once the glue is dry it will stay on underwater until the turtle comes back to its breeding beach in two or three years.

The journey

The tracker shows if the turtle's journey crosses fishing grounds, shipping routes and tourist areas. All these pose a danger to the turtle and may have to be moved to keep the turtles safe.

1 The turtle leaves the breeding beach with the tracker.

2 The turtle dives to find food but comes to the surface to breathe every 20 minutes.

3 At the surface, the tracker sends its position to a signal to a satellite.

GEOLOCATORS

Scientists can learn about animal movements by fitting geolocators. These little trackers do not send out signals showing locations. Instead they store useful information, which can be collected later.

POP-UP TAGS

Sea creatures, such as sharks, are always on the move and can dive to great depths – far too deep for signals from radio trackers to get through. Instead, scientists fit a type of geolocator called a tag tracker.

A great white shark is ready to be hoisted back into the water after a geolocator has been fitted to its **dorsal fin.**

FACT: Geolocators can weigh less than 1 gram (0.04 ounces) and keep running for 5 years.

Tag trackers record all kinds of **data**, such as light levels, saltiness and water depth. Once its memory is full, the tag is released from the animal and floats to the surface. It then uploads its data to a satellite, which transmits the information to the researchers.

LIGHT-LOGGERS

The smallest geolocators are fitted to birds. They are called light-loggers. They record when the sun rises and sets. Scientists have to recapture the bird to collect the data. Day lengths change depending on the location and time of year, and scientists use the data from the light-logger to track where the bird has been.

Light-logging geolocators, like those used on birds, get muddled by cloudy days. They are therefore less accurate than other trackers.

The geolocator on this shark's fin is covered in seaweed. The tag stays on for several months before coming off.

Diving with Elephant Seals

Elephant seals spend most of their time far out at sea. Data collection tags are used to find out more about how they live.

Northern elephant seals live in the northern Pacific ocean. They gather in large numbers on beaches to breed and give birth to their young. For 10 months of the year they are out of sight in the deep ocean.

Collecting facts

For the last 30 years scientists have been finding out about the life of elephant seals. They use tags that record different information. The latest tags are glued to the seal's head. They are geolocators that record light levels and water depths. This shows how deep seals dive to find food and how long they stay underwater. The tags also record the temperature of the water. They collect information about what the seal's body is doing, such as its heart rate. When the seal comes back to its breeding beach, researchers remove the tag.

Huge sea mammal

The elephant seal is so named for the trunk-like snout seen on the males. It is the largest type of seal. A male is 4 metres (14 feet) long. Females are a little shorter and much lighter in weight.

Life at sea

Trackers show that the seals from one beach usually stick together and live in the same part of the ocean all year. The male seals swim far from land. The females keep closer to the coast.

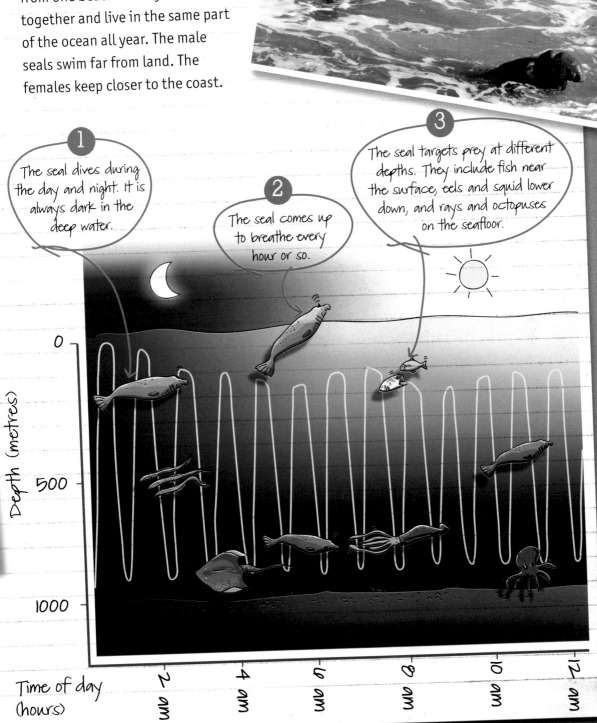

1 The seal dives during the day and night. It is always dark in the deep water.

2 The seal comes up to breathe every hour or so.

3 The seal targets prey at different depths. They include fish near the surface, eels and squid lower down, and rays and octopuses on the seafloor.

Depth (metres)

0

500

1000

Time of day (hours)

2 am 4 am 6 am 8 am 10 am 12 am

MAKING MARKINGS

Another way to keep track of animals does not need a lot of technology. Animals are simply tagged with an identifier that shows where they came from. Some animals can be identified by their **unique** markings.

IDENTITY TAGS

Numbered tags are used to track the movements of many animals, including fish, seals, butterflies and lobsters. However, the biggest tagging projects involve birds, which have small metal or plastic rings fitted to their legs.

A robin wears a tiny ring on its leg. This ring has a **unique** number that tells researchers where the bird came from.

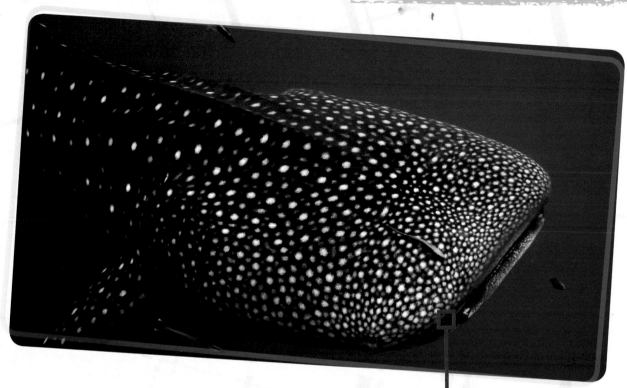

Whale sharks
have a unique
pattern of
spots. This
pattern can
be used to
identify them,
just like
a person's
fingerprint.

To fit a tag the animal must be caught. Before the tag is fitted the bird is weighed and measured. The tags are used to track migration routes and also to see how animals **disperse** as they look for new places to live. For the system to work, the animals must be re-caught so that their journeys can be recorded.

BIOMETRICS

Some animals can be identified without the need for tagging. They have unique marks already. Lions and dolphins, for example, can be identified by the scars they collect from fights. These unique patterns, called **biometrics**, can be recorded and used to identify animals whenever they are seen around the world.

FACT: An albatross ringed in 1956 was re-caught in 2014, making it the oldest wild bird ever recorded.

KEEPING UP WITH ZEBRAS

Computer technology is used to identify people from the shape of their face, the colour of their eyes or from their fingerprints. The technology can also track animals. One of the animals it works best on is the zebra.

When seen together, zebras all look much the same. However, their patterns of stripes are all unique.

IN THE CROWD

Zebras move in huge herds made up of hundreds or even thousands of animals. The zebras are often mixed in with antelopes, buffaloes and other **species**. A computer program developed by scientists in the United States and Africa makes it possible to identify zebras in the crowd.

TAKING PHOTOGRAPHS

The biometric system is called StripeCode. It does not need satellites or radio trackers to follow the herd. It just uses photographs and videos of the zebra herd taken in different places at different times. The computer scans the zebras' stripes, looking for patterns it has seen before and recording new ones to look for in other pictures.

WATCHING A HERD

The StripeCode system is helping to build up a picture of how a huge zebra herd moves. It might look like all the zebras go in the same direction at the same speed. However, the biometric tracker shows how the members of the herd are constantly being mixed up as some zebras run ahead and others fall behind.

WOW!

The zebra tracking software is very complicated. It is able to check its own results to ensure it does not count the same zebra twice or get mixed up between individuals. However, the basic idea is to convert a patch of zebra's fur into a pattern of dark dots. As long as the patch is big enough it will show a dot pattern that is unique to each zebra.

A computer turns a zebra's unique stripes into something like a bar code.

Ringing Songbirds

Bird ringing, or banding, happens all over the world. One of the projects is being run at Point Reyes in northern California.

Birds have been tracked from California's Palomarin Field Station for more than 50 years. In that time, the research has built up a detailed picture of how birds behave.

Migration watch

Many songbirds come to northern California to breed in summer. In winter they fly down the coast to where it is warmer. The Point Reyes bird ringing project tags 5,000 birds every year. When those birds migrate south in autumn, they are recaptured by other researchers along the way. Songbirds are very sensitive to changes to the **environment**. The number of birds can go up and down as their migration routes change. This information shows up problems in the environment, such as **pollution** or **climate change**.

mist nets

Birds are caught in mist nets. The nets are made from fine threads that the birds cannot see. The birds are not hurt by the net as long as they are removed carefully.

Taking details

As well as adding a ring, researchers measure the length of the bird's wings and tail and record its weight. If it is recaptured, the same things are checked, which shows if the bird has been feeding well on its journey. Any ringed birds that are found dead are also recorded.

3 The bird is caught again, and the ring shows where the bird came from.

2 The bird flies off, perhaps migrating to a warmer part of the world.

1 A bird is caught in a net and ringed.

The ring has a unique number.

UK 789

THE FUTURE

There is still a lot to learn about the movements of animals. Technology is making trackers smaller and more accurate. New techniques are being used to track animals of all kinds.

SMALLER AND BETTER

Scientists are always developing new ways to track animals that do not impact on their natural behaviour. For example, in 1890, Danish scientists began the first scientific tracking programme by fitting **zinc** rings to starlings. However, the bands were too heavy for the birds to fly. In 1899 a lighter metal – aluminium – became available and worked much better. Advances in technology are making today's trackers and geolocators small enough to fit on tiny animals. However, scientists are also using new tracking techniques.

This thrush has been fitted with a geolocator that is small and light in weight. In future full GPS trackers might be small enough for songbirds to carry.

NEW TECHNOLOGIES

Remote-controlled drone aircraft are used to follow big animals like elephants. Fish are being fitted with **acoustic** tags, which send out high-pitched beeps to show where they are. On a smaller scale, tiny bar codes are fitted to ants. The bar codes can be scanned by computers to see where the ants travel. Even weather **radar** is used to keep track of large flocks of birds and swarms of locusts. New techniques like these will reveal even more information about animals in the future.

Large flocks of migrating birds show up on weather radar designed to look for rain clouds.

NEXRAD Reflectivity (dBz)   0221 UTC 03 Oct. 2010 (09:21 PM CDT)

-5 0 5 10 15 20 25 30 35 40 45 50 55 60 65 70 75dBZ

GLOSSARY

acoustic to do with sound

biologist scientist who studies plants, animals and other living things

biometric measurement taken from a living body

bird of prey bird that hunts smaller animals to eat

climate change changes in weather conditions that scientists think are caused by changes humans make to Earth's atmosphere

data recorded facts normally listed as numbers. Scientists use data to find out something about the natural world.

disperse spread out

dorsal fin fin on the back of a fish or shark

environment surroundings or conditions in which a person, animal or plant lives or operates

habitat places where animals or plants live and grow

hibernate go into a deep sleep during winter

navigation finding out where you are and how to reach a destination

pollution something added to the environment that causes problems. Pollution can be chemicals in the air, soil or water.

population group of animals that live together and are distinct from other groups, at least some of the time

radar technology that bounces radio waves off objects and picks up any echoes. The system detects large objects that are too far away to see with the naked eye.

remotely controlled from a distance

satellite object that orbits (moves around) a larger one. Planets are satellites of the Sun and machines launched in orbit are also known as satellites.

sharpshooter accurate shooter who can hit targets a long distance away

species group of animals that can breed with each other

territory in biology this is a region controlled by an animal. The animal finds all its food in the territory and tries to stop other members of its species from living there.

unique unlike anything else

zinc silver-coloured metal

READ MORE

Amazing Animal Journeys (Great Migrations). Laura Marsh. Washington, D.C.: National Geographic Children's Books, 2010.

Animal Migrations (Epic!). Camilla de la Bedoyere. London: Wayland, 2015.

Animals, Tracks and Signs (Spotter's Guide). Alfred Leutscher and Sarah Kahn. London: Usborne, 2009.

Wildebeest (A Day in the Life: Grassland Animals). Louise Spilsbury. Oxford, UK: Raintree, 2011.

INTERNET SITES

Chesapeake Bay Foundation
A project for tracking ospreys.
www.cbf.org/ospreymap

Loch Garten Ospreys
This site includes a nestcam at Loch Garten.
http://www.rspb.org.uk/
discoverandenjoynature/seenature/
reserves/guide/l/lochgarten

Rutland Ospreys Project
Information about Rutland Water's ospreys.
www.ospreys.org.uk

Alaska Science Center (USGS)
Follow the polar bears of the Arctic Ocean.
alaska.usgs.gov/science/biology/polar_bears/tracking.html

INDEX